Yiddish Glossary and Pronunciation Guide

Yiddish is a language based on German that also incorporates Hebrew and Slavic words. It has been spoken by Jews around the world since at least the thirteenth century, though it is less common today than it was before World War II, during which millions of European Jews were murdered. Here are Yiddish words you will see throughout this story:

cheder (KHEH-dare; "kh" is similar to saying the sound of the letter "h" while gargling): elementary school

Mame (MA-meh): Mother

shtetl (SHTEH-tl): a small Jewish town in Eastern Europe

Tate (TAH-teh): Father

Zayde (ZAY-deh): Grandfather

To my parents, who taught me to ponder stories, art, Judaism, and justice
—C. L.

For my grandma, Lenore Dove Klein, for whom I drew each dove in this book
—E. T.

The illustrations for this book were made with gouache, acrylic, pencil, chalk, and linoleum block prints.

Cataloging-in-Publication Data has been applied for and may be obtained from the Library of Congress.

ISBN 978-1-4197-4130-2

Text copyright © 2021 Cynthia Levinson
Illustrations copyright © 2021 Evan Turk
Book design by Pamela Notarantonio

Printed and bound in China
10 9 8 7 6 5 4 3 2 1

Abrams Books for Young Readers are available at special discounts when purchased in quantity for premiums and promotions as well as fundraising or educational use. Special editions can also be created to specification. For details, contact specialsales@abramsbooks.com or the address below.

Abrams® is a registered trademark of Harry N. Abrams, Inc.

ABRAMS The Art of Books
195 Broadway, New York, NY 10007
abramsbooks.com

THE PEOPLE'S PAINTER
HOW BEN SHAHN FOUGHT FOR JUSTICE WITH ART

BY CYNTHIA LEVINSON
PICTURES BY EVAN TURK

Abrams Books for Young Readers • New York

"The first thing I can remember," Ben said, "I drew."

From the time he could grasp a pencil, Ben Shahn yearned to draw everything he saw in his village in Lithuania.

His mame Gittel's hands molding sturdy plates from slippery clay.

His tate Hessel carving stout chairs out of spruce trees.

And his tate's tate, Zayde, chiseling wooden skates so Ben could skim across the frozen Neris River.

But paper was a luxury in the shtetl, and there was none to spare. So, with his finger, Ben traced the Hebrew letters that curled and curved through his book of Bible stories. Then—he couldn't stop himself—he sketched in the margins!

Some Bible stories, though, enraged Ben—especially when good people got hurt. That's not right!

Ben also protested when his cheder teacher wasn't fair. After a classmate pulled a prank, the teacher kept everyone indoors, demanding the culprit's name.

"I'm not going to tell who did it," Ben declared, "and I'm not going to pay for something I didn't do." Refusing to tattle, he walked out.

Justice had mattered to Ben ever since he was little. He was only four when Czar Nicholas II's soldiers hurled rocks through his window and dragged his father away. Just because Tate had been demanding fair pay for working people, he was banished to frigid, far-off Siberia.

Ben didn't know yet how to draw his outrage. But, feeling his father's boldness inside himself, he marched up to the sentry at the end of the street and shouted, "Down with the Czar!"

The soldier chased after him, but Ben escaped.

Tate eventually escaped too, and in 1906, he made his way from Siberia to America. He wrote to Gittel: *Come.*

Eight-year-old Ben, his brother Philip, his sister Hattie, and his mame packed their belongings. But Zayde could not leave the shtetl, the only home he knew.

As the stagecoach pulled away, Ben had to let go of his grandfather's hand. He wailed.

America bewildered the new immigrant.
Trains overhead and underground.

A cramped two-room tenement apartment for the whole family.

A chair that rocked and nearly dumped him over backwards—not at all like Tate's.

Tomatoes—ick!

And in school, Ben stared at what seemed like thousands of letters in all different shapes and styles and sizes. All different from Hebrew. Even worse, bullies tormented him about his clothes and accent, and they called him names just because he was Jewish.

Sometimes, though, they'd pause if he chalked their portraits on the sidewalk. No one drew people better than Ben.

Seeing his craving to draw, a teacher gave him watercolors. Another paid him to pen calligraphy—elegantly curving letters, all in English. By the time he was twelve, Ben was determined to become an artist.

To do that, he'd need to finish high school; go to college; learn about colors, lines, anatomy. But his father lost his job, and when Ben turned fourteen, his mother ordered him to leave school and go to work. He argued bitterly, *Send Philip, instead!* But his family needed whatever Ben could earn.

So he apprenticed to a lithographer, who hand-lettered signs for billboards and chiseled them into stone storefronts. By day, Ben carefully copied those thousands of English letters. He spent months on *a*, tracing and carving every curl and curve. Then, he moved on to *b*. Gradually, he fell in love with these letters, too. After five years, he mastered the craft, and his signs began to appear around the city.

Meanwhile, at night, Ben went to art school, hoping to perfect his portraits. But there was a problem. Ben's teachers taught landscapes. Purple-shadowed valleys, misty haystacks, fields of cows. Ben argued that shadows are not purple. And he detested cows!

"I like stories and people," he explained. Stories about people fighting injustice, about workers like Tate, loved ones like Zayde, and immigrants like himself. His teachers, though, insisted that paintings weren't supposed to tell stories. That pictures should be beautiful—not real life.

Since he didn't want to portray pleasant pastures or cows, Ben wondered if he was an artist after all. Maybe he should only make signs. Nearly thirty years old now, confused and discouraged, he quit school, stopped painting, and sailed to Europe, then on to Africa. In museums, he gazed at centuries of pictures.

"This may be art but is it my own art?" he pondered.

During that time, protests over an unfair trial in America also caught Ben's eye. Two Italian American men, Nicola Sacco and Bartolomeo Vanzetti, were executed in 1927 for a murder they probably did not commit. The judge and jury believed they must be guilty, since they were poor immigrants and they opposed democracy.

"Here was something to paint!" Ben later exclaimed, infuriated at the injustice. "If I am to be a painter, I must show the world how it looks through my eyes, not theirs. What shall I paint? Stories."

He returned home and told their tale in twenty-three pictures—even though his teachers had insisted that he must not tell stories. And people flocked to see them, even if they weren't pretty.

Ben didn't stop there. He painted other stories about outsiders: working people, prisoners, and Jews who had been mistreated, just like Tate. His portraits were so powerful that in 1935, the United States government hired him. It was the Great Depression, and jobs were scarce. So was food. President Franklin D. Roosevelt wanted Americans to see that poor people needed a helping hand from Washington.

For this job, instead of painting on canvas, Ben borrowed a camera. With his friend Bernarda Bryson, whom he later married, he crisscrossed the countryside taking photographs that revealed hard lives in troubled times.

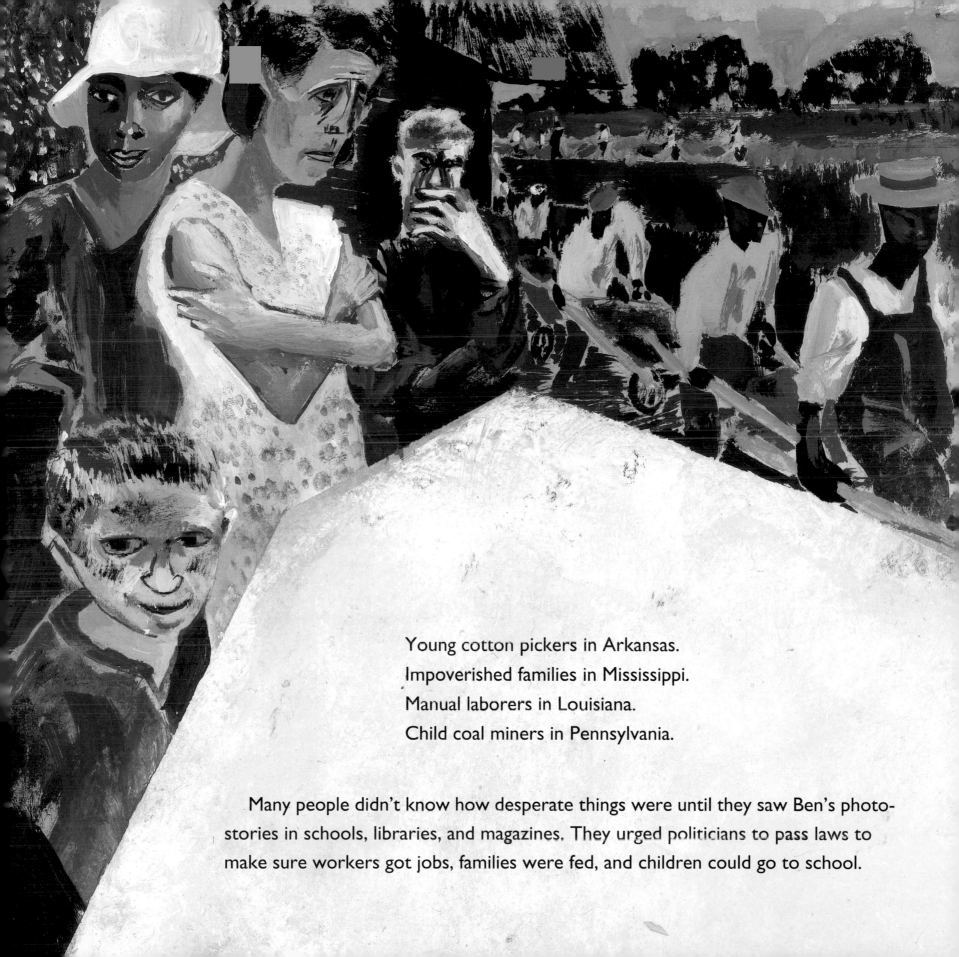

Young cotton pickers in Arkansas.
Impoverished families in Mississippi.
Manual laborers in Louisiana.
Child coal miners in Pennsylvania.

Many people didn't know how desperate things were until they saw Ben's photo-stories in schools, libraries, and magazines. They urged politicians to pass laws to make sure workers got jobs, families were fed, and children could go to school.

The government hired Ben again in 1937, this time to paint a mural in a new village named Jersey Homesteads. President Roosevelt's New Deal program had built the town so garment workers, most of them Jewish, could move from city tenements to the airy countryside. What story would Ben tell? His own!

In three scenes, he showed immigrants—
including Mame—arriving poor and
bewildered in America, working hard,
demanding fair pay, and, finally, settling happily
in Jersey Homesteads.

To Ben, the village felt like a shtetl! He and
Bernarda liked it so much, they moved there.
Their children walked by the mural at school
every day.

While some parts of the government displayed Ben's works, others didn't trust him. In the 1940s and 1950s, congressmen accused him of being disloyal because he didn't paint purple mountain majesties or America the beautiful. Instead, he shed light on Americans who lived in the shadows.

One wintry day, two men appeared at Ben's door and flashed their IDs: Federal Bureau of Investigation. They questioned him relentlessly.

Why do you support workers? Immigrants? Civil rights?

Isn't America fine the way it is?

Which of your friends are enemies of America?

Ben politely served them tea and cake, but he refused to tattle. So the FBI threatened to deport him to Lithuania, just as the Czar had exiled Tate to Siberia!

But Ben was not disloyal. "I am the most American of all American painters," he later said. Eventually, the FBI backed down.

Anyway, threats had never scared Ben. "I hate injustice," he had declared.

For the next sixteen years, Ben continued
to portray stories of people clamoring for
their rights.

Civil rights activists.

Workers demanding fair pay.

Political protesters.

Advocates for peace.

Americans loved Ben's art so much, they
called him "the people's painter."

Ben drew until the end of his life, handing down
his stories of justice from generation to generation.
When he was a zayde himself, Ben encouraged
young artists to sketch anywhere.

Especially in the margins.

Author's Note

Ben Shahn was so concerned about what was happening around him that you could almost track American history from the early 1900s to the 1960s through his work. In addition to the issues raised in this book, he addressed both world wars, Social Security, the Dust Bowl, nuclear arms testing, voting rights, the Vietnam War, and health care.

Art that focuses on current events is called "social realism." Some congressmen considered Ben's artwork in this style unpatriotic, and he was investigated by the House Un-American Activities Committee. Nevertheless, Ben's social realist pieces are still displayed in government buildings and universities.

Hugely popular, Ben was one of the youngest artists to have a retrospective exhibit at the Museum of Modern Art in New York City. His shows at art galleries routinely sold out, and he was hired to create pieces for a wide variety of purposes.

Ben also sketched greeting cards, posters, advertisements, and record jackets. He decorated shipping containers, a Passover Haggadah, and stage sets for ballets, and he created stained glass windows for a synagogue. He designed lettering in several alphabets and wrote a book titled *Love and Joy About Letters*. Ben illustrated stories for teenagers' magazines and his drawings were even used in a children's book called *Ounce, Dice, Trice*. As a photographer, he sometimes used a right-angle camera, which allowed him to face in one direction while snapping a picture of an unsuspecting subject in another!

In 1922, Ben married Tillie Goldstein, with whom he had two children. Ten years later, while painting a mural with Diego Rivera, Ben met Bernarda Bryson, a journalist and artist. Ben divorced Tillie; he and Bernarda later married and raised their three children in Jersey Homesteads. In 1945, Ben helped change the town's name to Roosevelt, in honor of President Franklin Delano Roosevelt. School children there still study Ben's mural. One wrote in a report, "You just have to look at it, and you see the story."

I have long been drawn to Ben Shahn because of his fervent style, incorporation of Jewish themes, and focus on social justice. My interest bourgeoned when I met Bernarda Bryson Shahn in 1993 and discovered that we had attended the same high school in Columbus, Ohio, about four decades apart. Through talking with her, their son Jonathan, and others, and by studying his art, I came to appreciate what Ben once told his student, children's author and illustrator Tomie dePaola: "Being an artist is not only what you do, but also how you live your life."

In addition to the people I interviewed, I am indebted to Lyudmila Sholokhova, then at the YIVO Institute for Jewish Research, Marisa Bourgoin at the Smithsonian Institution, Janet Evans Brady at Harvard University, Susan Edwards at the Frist Center for the Visual Arts, Chris Glass of the Boston Public Library, Susan Wallner at NJN Public Television and Radio, and Chris Barton and Erin Murphy as well as my dear editor Emma Ledbetter—who as a child attended a synagogue containing art installations by Shahn—her insightful assistant Sara Sproull, and the brilliant Evan Turk. My children and grandchildren are as thoroughly splendid as ever.

—C. L.

Illustrator's Note

Ben Shahn has been one of my favorite artists for a long time. I even did a project on one of his Sacco and Vanzetti paintings when I was in fifth grade! I admire the bold shapes and rich textures he uses, as well as the very spontaneous and expressive way he drew people. He didn't try to create exact likenesses of people, but tried to capture the way they felt and exaggerated to help tell the story more clearly. I wanted to bring a lot of his influence into the illustrations I made for this book. The paintings for this book were created mostly in gouache (a kind of opaque watercolor) with little bits of pencil, chalk, acrylic paint, and linoleum block printing. I also used a lot of masking tape to make the crisp lines and shapes. I always loved that Ben Shahn's paintings told stories, and I think telling his story with paintings, and Cynthia's beautiful words, is a perfect tribute to one of the United States' most influential illustrators.

—E. T.

Timeline

Year	Snapshots of Ben Shahn's Life	The Bigger Picture
1898	Ben Shahn was born to Hessel and Gittel Shahn in Kovno, Lithuania.	Lithuania was part of the Pale of Settlement, the area within the Russian Empire where Jews were allowed to live.
1902	Hessel was exiled to Siberia.	Czar Nicholas II ordered pogroms—attacks—against Jews in the Pale of Settlement.
1906	Ben and his family immigrated to New York City.	Around a million immigrants entered the United States through Ellis Island.
1913	Ben began apprenticing at his uncle's lithography shop while studying art at night.	
1920s	Ben married Tillie Goldstein. They traveled in Europe and Morocco.	
1930s	Ben painted a series on Sacco and Vanzetti.	Worldwide protests occurred over concerns that Sacco and Vanzetti were executed because they were immigrants and anarchists.
	The US government hired Ben to photograph poverty in America.	The Depression, along with the Dust Bowl in the Midwest, caused widespread poverty, unemployment, loss of farmland, and hunger. President Roosevelt worked to improve the economy through government programs called the New Deal.
	Ben divorced Tillie and later married Bernarda Bryson. He painted a fresco at Jersey Homesteads where they lived.	The New Deal built settlements in rural areas to reduce urban crowding and poverty.
1940s	Ben designed posters for the Office of War Information.	The United States fought with the Allies in World War II from 1941 to 1945.
	Ben created artwork to promote labor unions, voting rights, and a ban on nuclear bombs.	
	The Museum of Modern Art held a retrospective of Ben's works.	
1950s	The FBI and the House Un-American Activities Committee investigated Ben's political views.	Politicians raised alarms, with no evidence, about a spread of communism in America.
1960s	Ben portrayed heroes of the civil rights movement.	Calls for civil rights and voting rights spread.
	Ben designed anti-war images.	The US fought in wars in Southeast Asia.
1969	Ben died on March 14.	

Selected Bibliography

Books

Bush, Martin H. *Ben Shahn: The Passion of Sacco and Vanzetti*. Syracuse, NY: Syracuse University Press, 1968.

Chevlowe, Susan. *Common Man, Mythic Vision: The Paintings of Ben Shahn*. Princeton, NJ: Princeton University Press, 1998.

Greenfeld, Howard. *Ben Shahn: An Artist's Life*. New York: Random House, 1998.

Katzman, Laura. *Drawing on the Left: Ben Shahn and the Art of Human Rights*. Harrisonburg, VA: Duke Hall Gallery of Fine Arts, James Madison University, 2017.

Library of Congress. *Fields of Vision: The Photographs of Ben Shahn*. Introduction by Timothy Egan. Washington, DC: Library of Congress, 2008.

Linden, Diana L. *Ben Shahn's New Deal Murals*. Detroit, MI: Wayne State University Press, 2015.

Morse, John D., ed. *Ben Shahn*. New York: Praeger Publishers, 1972.

Pohl, Frances K. *Ben Shahn: New Deal Artist in a Cold War Climate, 1947–1954*. Austin, TX: University of Texas Press 1989.

———. *Ben Shahn with Ben Shahn's Writings*. San Francisco, CA: Pomegranate Artbooks, 1993.

Prescott, Kenneth W. *The Complete Graphic Works of Ben Shahn*. New York: Quadrangle/The New York Times Book Co., 1973.

Reid, Alastair. *Ounce Dice Trice*. Boston, MA: Little, Brown & Company, 1958.

Rodman, Selden. *Portrait of the Artist as an American, Ben Shahn: A Biography with Pictures*. New York: Harper & Brothers Publishers, 1951.

Shahn, Ben. *Love and Joy About Letters*. New York: Grossman Publishers, 1963.

———. *The Shape of Content*. Cambridge, MA: Harvard University Press, 1957.

Soby, James Thrall. *Ben Shahn*. New York: Museum of Modern Art, Penguin Books, 1947. See moma.org/documents/moma_catalogue_3216_300170615.pdf.

———. *Ben Shahn: His Graphic Art*. New York: George Braziller, Inc., 1957.

———. *Ben Shahn: Paintings*. New York: George Braziller, Inc., 1963.

Personal Interviews

Bernarda Bryson Shahn, artist and wife of Ben Shahn

Tomie dePaola, artist and student of Ben Shahn

Ilene Levine, teacher at Roosevelt Public School

Diana Linden, Shahn scholar

Alan Mallach, secretary, Roosevelt Arts Project

Frances Pohl, professor of art history, Pomona College

Laura Rhondah Katzman, professor of art history, James Madison University

Mary Robinson Cohen, superintendent of Roosevelt Public School

Jonathan Shahn, sculptor and son of Ben Shahn

Site Visits

Central US Post Office, The Bronx, New York City

Roosevelt Public School, Roosevelt, New Jersey

Voice of America (originally the Social Security Administration), Washington, DC

Whitney Museum of American Art, New York City

Websites

Archives of American Art, aaa.si.edu/collections/ben-shahn-papers-6935

Archives of American Art, Oral history interview with Ben Shahn by Forrest Selvig, September 27, 1968, aaa.si.edu/collections/interviews/oral-history-interview-ben-shahn-13314#transcript

ArtCyclopedia, artcyclopedia.com/artists/shahn_ben.html

State of the Arts—New Jersey, "Ben Shahn: Passion for Justice" (film), youtube.com/watch?v=LFYwcq0veXc

Source Notes

p. 5   "The first thing . . . I drew." Radio interview by Nadya Aisenberg, WGBH Radio, Boston, 1957, as quoted in Morse, *Ben Shahn*, 42.

p. 11   "I'm not . . . I didn't do." Oral history interview with Ben Shahn, September 27, 1968. Archives of American Art, Smithsonian Institution. See aaa.si.edu/collections/interviews/oral-history-interview-ben-shahn-13314.

p. 14   "Down with the Czar!" Pohl, *Ben Shahn with Ben Shahn's Writings*, 7.

p. 29   "I like stories and people." Soby, *Ben Shahn*, 6.

p. 31   "This may be art but is it my own art?" Rodman, *Portrait of the Artist as an American, Ben Shahn: A Biography with Pictures*, 117.

p. 33   "Here was something to paint!" Soby, *Ben Shahn: Paintings*, 11.

p. 33   "If I am . . . not theirs." The Art Story, "Ben Shahn Paintings, Bio, Ideas." See theartstory.org/artist/shahn-ben/.

p. 33   "What shall I paint? Stories." Artcyclopedia, "Ben Shahn," quoted by Katherine Kuh. See artcyclopedia.com/artists/shahn_ben.html.

p. 40   "I am . . . painters." Oral history interview with Ben Shahn, September 27, 1968. Archives of American Art, Smithsonian Institution. See aaa.si.edu/collections/interviews/oral-history-interview-ben-shahn-13314.

p. 40   "I hate injustice." Greenfeld, *Ben Shahn: An Artist's Life*, 8.

p. 43   "people's painter." Linden, *Ben Shahn's New Deal Murals*, 77.

p. 46   "You just have . . . the story." Elizabeth Stinson, "The History of Roosevelt: What We Learned from Mrs. Chasan and Mrs. Shahn," Fourth Grade, Roosevelt Public School, 1996.

p. 46   "Being an artist . . . your life." Telephone interview with Tomie de Paola, September 15, 2015.